Woo-hoo!

Name:

....

Birthday:

....

Favorite holiday:

....

Hooray!

National Bird Day

Feed the birds

WHAT YOU NEED
birdseed
empty toilet paper roll
peanut butter
twine

1.

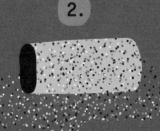

Spread peanut butter on the outside of an empty toilet paper roll.

2.

Roll it in birdseed.

3.

Use twine to hang it outdoors.

4.

Observe the birds that visit your feeder, and jot down what you notice and what you wonder.

Peep a bird cam

Do some virtual bird-watching at cams.allaboutbirds.org. The Cornell Lab of Ornithology provides links to live bird cams around the world.

The average hummingbird weighs less than a nickel.

5¢

When it's looking for food, the Australian Bassian Thrush farts at the ground to reveal worms to eat.

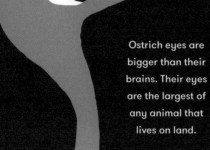

Ostrich eyes are bigger than their brains. Their eyes are the largest of any animal that lives on land.

Family birding

Go for a bird walk with this book. Draw every bird you see. If you need help identifying them, check out a nature guide or allaboutbirds.org.

Bird name: ....

Bird name: ....

Bird name: ....

Bird name: ....

Create your own bird species

Bird name: ....

Static Electricity Day

Have you ever had a hair-raising experience after taking off your winter hat? Or when shuffling across the carpet, have you touched a doorknob and felt a shock?

That's static electricity.

Here's how it works:

This is an atom.

It is a super-small particle that makes up everything in the universe.

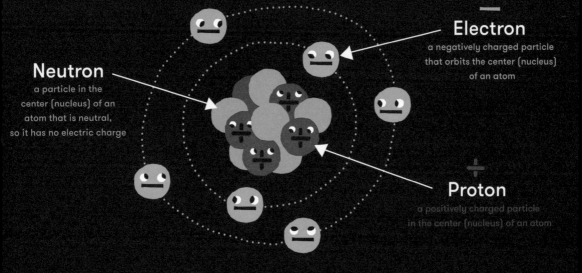

Electron
a negatively charged particle
that orbits the center (nucleus)
of an atom

Neutron
a particle in the
center (nucleus) of an
atom that is neutral,
so it has no electric charge

Proton
a positively charged particle
in the center (nucleus) of an atom

The imbalance of positive and negative charges on an object is static electricity.

Objects that have an equal amount of
protons and electrons are "balanced."

When certain objects rub together, electrons
from one object can move to another object.

This causes the object that loses electrons to
be positively charged and the object that
gains the electrons to be negatively charged.

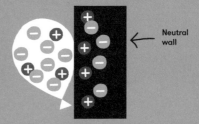

Neutral
wall

Opposite charges attract each other, and like
charges repel each other. Both types of charges
will attract a neutral object (with no charge).

Balloon experiment

1. Charge one balloon by rubbing it on your head.

2. Put the charged side against a wall.

What happens?

3.

Put the charged balloon
against the second balloon.

What happens?

4. Charge both balloons and put them together.

What happens?

So what's happening here?

Rubbing the balloon with your hair gives it a
negative charge, causing it to stick to neutrally
charged surfaces, such as a wall or a non-charged
balloon. Eventually the static charge dissipates, and
the balloon loses its charge, so it no longer sticks.

When both balloons are negatively charged,
they repel each other.

You'll be shocked (get it?) at how easy it is!

Make a rad shirt

1. Draw a lightning-bolt shape on the sponge.

2. Use the scissors to cut out the lightning-bolt shape.

3. Generously coat one side of the lightning bolt with fabric paint.

4. Stamp away! Put as many bolts as you like on your shirt. Reapply paint in between each stamping.

5. Allow the paint to dry before rockin' your new shirt!

What is lightning?

Lightning is similar to static electricity, but on a much bigger scale. In a thunderstorm, water droplets in the clouds collide with one another, releasing electrons and building up an electric charge. That charge may jump to earth as a bolt of lightning.

Make lightning in a jar

Try this on a day with low humidity.

WHAT YOU NEED

jar with a metal cap

aluminum foil

scissors

5 or 6 thumbtacks

dryer sheet

inflated balloon

1.

Create the anode.

This is the positively charged electrode toward which electrons will flow.

Cut a piece of aluminum foil into a 12" x 12" square. Fold it over twice into a smaller square and push it into the bottom of the jar.

2.

Create the cathode.

This is the negatively charged electrode from which electrons will flow.

Push the thumbtacks through a dryer sheet so their heads are facing the top of the jar. Put the dryer sheet over the mouth of the jar and screw on the lid.

3.

Charge the balloon.

Rub the balloon on your head.

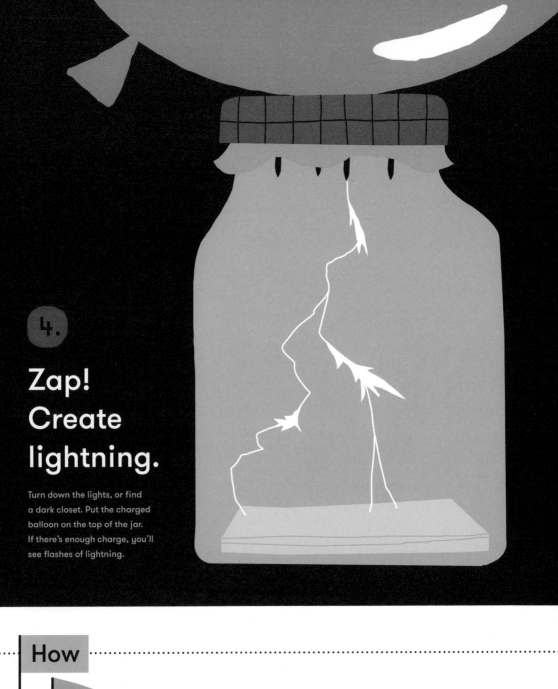

4.

Zap!
Create
lightning.

Turn down the lights, or find
a dark closet. Put the charged
balloon on the top of the jar.
If there's enough charge, you'll
see flashes of lightning.

How

we

celebrated

National Popcorn Day

Why does popcorn pop?

Popcorn has small kernels with hard outer shells. If you heat the kernel, the moisture inside it turns to steam. And when the outer shell has reached its pressure point, it bursts. POP!

Popcorn toss

1. Label 4 large cups with 5, 20, 50, and 100, and place them on a table.

like this

2. Set a chair a few feet back.

3. Each player takes turns sitting in the chair and tossing 10 pieces of popped popcorn into the cups. Add up the scores based on how many pieces land in the cups.

Movie night popcorn party

Gather some family or friends, turn on a favorite movie, and put out a big bowl of popcorn and lots of possible toppings.

| pretzel sticks | chocolate chips | roasted nuts | dried cherries | coconut flakes | cinnamon |

make sure no one's allergic

Draw a scene from your favorite movie.
See if anyone can guess what movie it is from.

NOW PLAYING

How

we

celebrated

National Measure Your Feet Day

My feet

Trace them here.

Left foot length: ....

Right foot length: ....

Use this ruler to measure. ⟶

9 8 7 6 5 4 3 2 1

My family's feet

Name:	left foot length:
Name:	left foot length:
Name:	left foot length:
Name:	left foot length:

Whoever has the shortest foot, give everyone a high five (with your foot)!

Total number of toes in my family
(include pets if you have them):

Foot facts

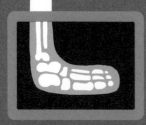

One quarter of your body's bones are in your feet.

Your feet have 250,000 sweat glands. (P.U.)

In your lifetime, you'll probably take enough steps to circle the Earth almost 5 times.

Guess whose footprint [not actual size]

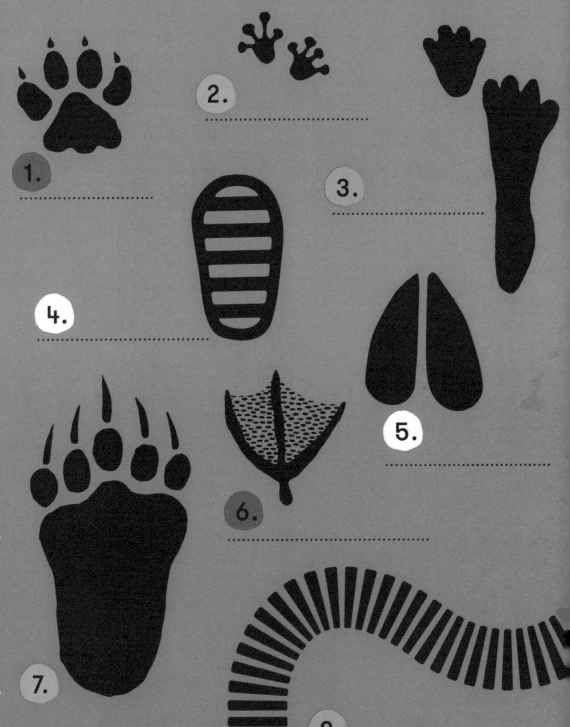

National Backward Day

TIP: Having trouble reading?
Hold this page up to a mirror.

My name spelled backward:

We're celebrating everything backward today. Ready to reverse your ways?

Some ideas

Wear your shirt backward

Greet people by saying "goodbye!"

Eat breakfast for dinner

Call everyone by their last name

Write backward
(maybe not in your school assignment)

Walk backward
(careful!)

Play a board game from finish to start

What else?

....

....

....

....

....

Send a
Card
to a
Friend
Day

Today's a really good day to let your friends know you're thinking about them.

A few of my friends:

Why they are awesome:

....

....

....

....

....

....

....

....

....

....

....

Use the 2 postcards
in the back of this book!

POST

Make Up Your Own Holiday Day

What do you think deserves a little more consideration? Whether meaningful, funny, or just really weird, now's your chance to celebrate whatever you choose!

What's the name of your holiday?

What date will you celebrate it?

What it celebrates

Ways to celebrate
(activities, food, decorations, and more)

Why it's worth celebrating

National Find a Rainbow Day

How it works:

Sunlight is a mix of all the rainbow colors. When light refracts (bends) through water (like a raindrop), the light disperses, and you can see the spectrum of colors that make up a rainbow.

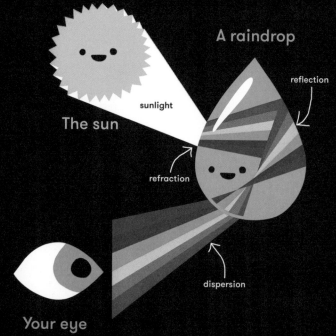

The sun

sunlight

A raindrop

reflection

refraction

dispersion

Your eye

Look outside.
See a rainbow?
If not, make
your own!

1. Put the mirror in the glass of water at an angle.

2. Position the glass so that sunlight shines on the mirror.

3. Find a reflection on the wall.

4. Adjust the angle of the mirror until a rainbow appears.

sunlight

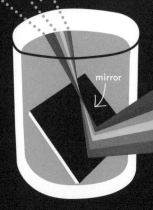

mirror

Today's a good day to wear the colors of the rainbow. Color in the best R-O-Y-G-B-I-V* outfit you can imagine.

My favorite color is rainbow

Find the rainbow stickers in the back of this book. Hide a few in plain sight, and brighten someone's day.

Eat a rainbow

Make a colorful surprise for dinner tonight!

Name the colors of the rainbow: ROYGBIV

National Haiku Poetry Day

A haiku is a form of Japanese poetry with three lines.

The first line has 5 syllables, then 7 syllables, then 5 more.

Traditionally, haikus were about nature—but you can make yours about whatever you want.

Write a haiku about a pickle.

Title: ....

....
5 syllables

....
7 syllables

....
5 syllables

At dinner

Ask everyone to come up with
a haiku about their day...
or about the person seated
to their right.

Surprise in the mail

Write a haiku to someone special,
signed "your secret admirer,"
and send it to them.

Another haiku:

....
5 syllables

....
7 syllables

....
5 syllables

Morse Code Day

Before the telephone or email was invented, the Morse code allowed people to communicate long distances almost instantly by electric telegraph.

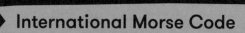

International Morse Code

A ●—		N —●	T —
B —●●●	H ●●●●	O ———	U ●●—
C —●—●	I ●●	P ●——●	V ●●●—
D —●●	J ●———	Q ——●—	W ●——
E ●	K —●—	R ●—●	X —●●—
F ●●—●	L ●—●●	S ●●●	Y —●——
G ——●	M ——		Z ——●●

How it works

By tapping out messages using the code, electrical signals are transmitted over a wire. On the other end, a receiver beeps out the code, and operators can translate the message.

Dit

Dah

My name in Morse code is:

Decode this message:

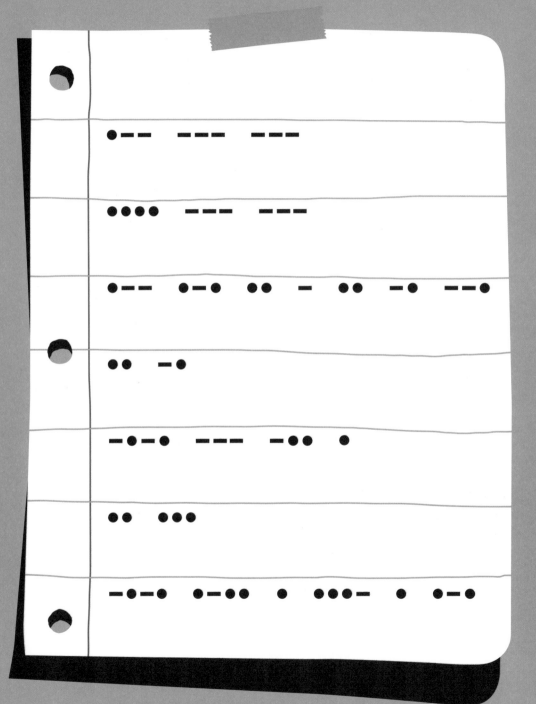

Create your own code

Make symbols for each character in the alphabet. Then share it with
a friend, and send them a secret message written entirely in code.

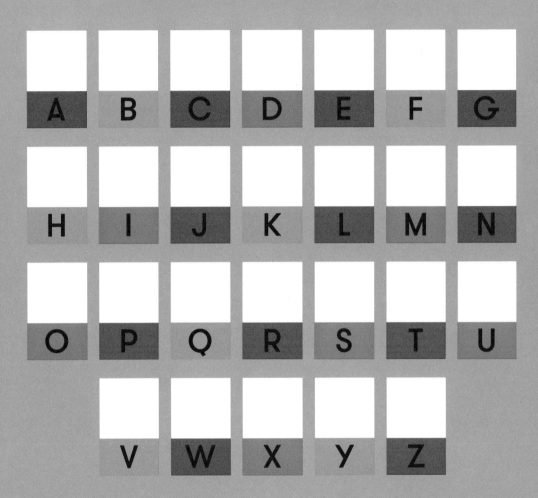

A B C D E F G

H I J K L M N

O P Q R S T U

V W X Y Z

**Have you heard of the SOS
distress signal?** ●●● ─── ●●●

The *Titanic* transmitted this signal before it sank.

Hug Your Cat Day

Studies show that petting a
cat can have a positive, calming effect.
Don't have a furry feline? Don't worry.
There are still ways to celebrate.

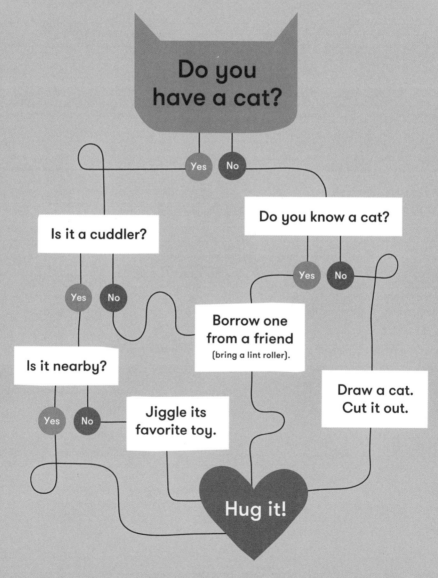

Do you have a cat?

Yes / No

Is it a cuddler?

Yes / No

Do you know a cat?

Yes / No

Borrow one from a friend (bring a lint roller).

Is it nearby?

Yes / No

Jiggle its favorite toy.

Draw a cat. Cut it out.

Hug it!

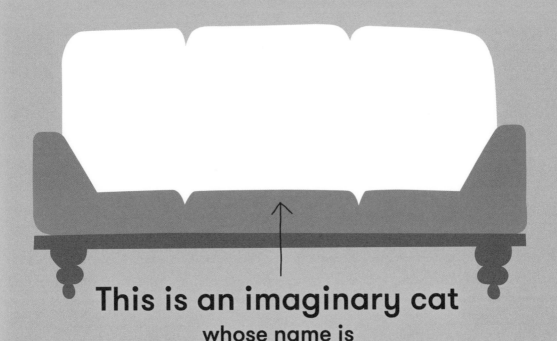

This is an imaginary cat

whose name is

and who ....

....

Cat Fact:

Just like you have a fingerprint that no one else has, cats have unique nose prints.

Origa-meow!

Cut a piece of paper into a 5"x 5" square, and fold like this:

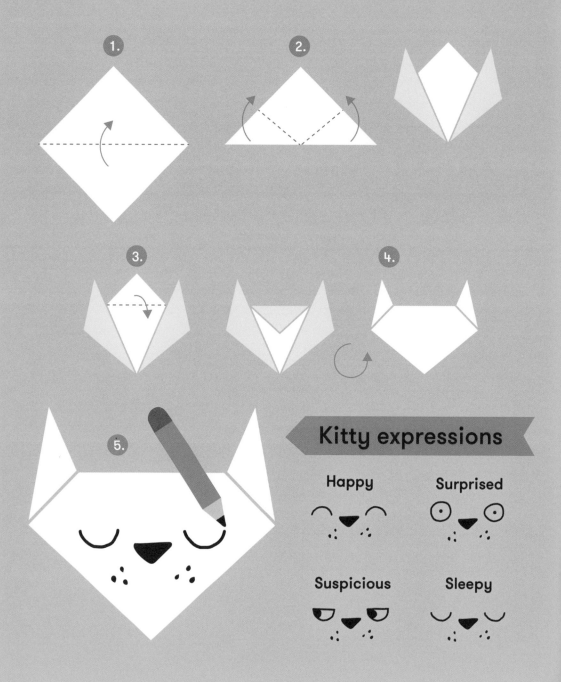

Kitty expressions

Happy

Surprised

Suspicious

Sleepy

Put a hat on this cat
(not just a normal hat).

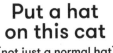

Field trip!

Visit a local shelter for a feline fix, and spend some time there volunteering.

Cutest cat video contest

Family game

1. Split into teams.
2. Give each team 3 minutes to find the cutest possible cat video on the internet.
3. Get back together to watch.
4. Awwww.

How we celebrated

National Tell a Joke Day

For more
puns, check out
the book
wee *heehee*
A Collection of
Pretty Funny Jokes
& Pictures.

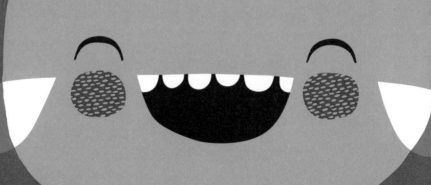

How to tell a joke

1.

Practice.

Read the joke out loud a few times
until you remember it.
Then try it in front of a mirror.

2.

Ask first.

Find a friend or family member and ask,
"Want to hear a joke?"
(They'll almost always say yes.)

3.

Set it up.

As you start the joke, make sure
you're slow and clear, so they
understand every word.

4.

Pause.

This is the toughest part, especially
when you're nervous or excited.
But the pause creates suspense
and makes the joke much funnier.

5.

Punch line!

Slowly and clearly deliver the punch line.

Then wait for the laughs. If it's a bust,
move on—try another joke.
You can do it. You're hilarious.

Who lived next
door to the horse?
His neigh-bor!

Knock, knock.
Who's there?
Lettuce.
Lettuce who?
Lettuce in!
It's cold outside.

Where do
basketball
players sleep?
In dunk beds.

What do you
call a train
that's under
the weather?
Ahh-choo choo.

Why did the bear have
trouble watching the video?

He kept pressing paws!

Reactions I've gotten when I tell this joke:

Name: _____   Date: _____

- ☐ snort-laugh
- ☐ guffaw
- ☐ polite grin
- ☐ delayed chuckle
- ☐ giggles
- ☐ confusion
- ☐ head shake
- ☐ nada

Name: _____   Date: _____

- ☐ snort-laugh
- ☐ guffaw
- ☐ polite grin
- ☐ delayed chuckle
- ☐ giggles
- ☐ confusion
- ☐ head shake
- ☐ nada

Name: _____   Date: _____

- ☐ snort-laugh
- ☐ guffaw
- ☐ polite grin
- ☐ delayed chuckle
- ☐ giggles
- ☐ confusion
- ☐ head shake
- ☐ nada

This person has the best laugh:
_____

It sounds a little like a:
_____

National Read a Book Day

Today's the day to curl up with a good book.
See if you can get in some extra reading time.

A few more ideas

Shake it up

Do you usually stick with the same genre? There's a whole world of books to explore. Head to the library and pick out something you wouldn't normally choose. If you get stuck, ask someone for a recommendation.

Family book club

Get everybody on the same page this month. Pick out a crowd-pleaser, and read the same book at the same time. Then plan a special book club dinner to discuss it together. Come up with a few thought-starter questions ahead of time.

Get outside

There's something special about reading outside. Bring your book to a park, or the beach, or your front stoop. It's even better with a snack. Busy with school today? Make a plan for this weekend.

My favorite books

1st

Title:

By:

What I loved about it:

2nd

Title:

By:

What I loved about it:

3rd

Title:

By:

What I loved about it:

Make and share corner bookmarks

Cut a piece of paper into a 5"x5" square, and fold like this:

1.

2.

3.

4.

5.

6.

Cut and glue on shapes for eyes, ears, a nose, a mouth, or whatever else you come up with.

Talk Like a Pirate Day

Ahoy! My pirate name be:

SOME IDEAS

Pirate Kate Crazy Eye

Pirate Sid Soggybritches

Cap'n Yellowbeard

....

Try talking like a pirate all day long. Or maybe just during dinner?
Be sure to give everyone in your family a pirate name.
And if you're talking like a pirate, you may as well dress like one.

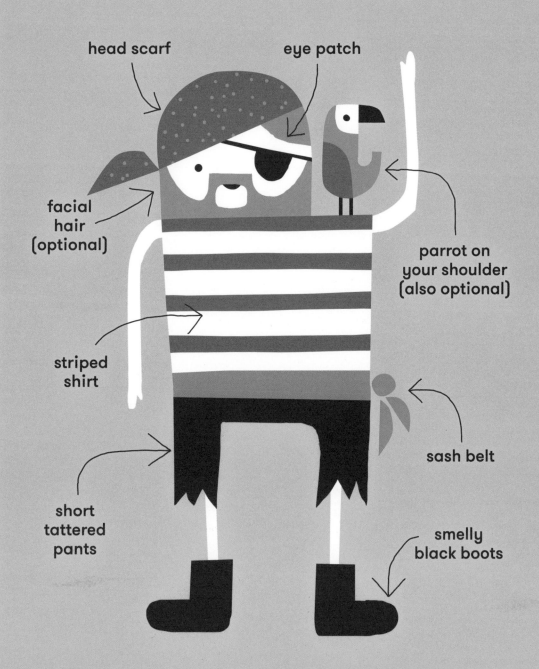

head scarf

eye patch

facial
hair
(optional)

parrot on
your shoulder
(also optional)

striped
shirt

sash belt

short
tattered
pants

smelly
black boots

How do you talk like a pirate?

It's mostly in your attitude and tone—kinda growly.
And here are some key pirate words and phrases.
For more help, search for "pirate translator" or "pirate dictionary" online.

Ahoy, matey

Blimey!

Ahoy, matey
Hello, friend

All hands on deck!
An urgent request for all crew to come to the deck to help

Argh!
Argh!

Avast!
Stop!

Aye!
Yes, or I agree

Batten down the hatches
Prepare for rough seas

Blimey!
An expression of surprise

Booty
Pirate's treasure

Buccaneer
Pirate

Doubloon
Gold coin found in pirate treasure

Fire in the hole
Warning before a cannon is fired

Hornswoggle
Trick or deceive someone

Jolly Roger
The pirate flag with a skull and crossbones

Land, ho!
An exclamation to use when you first spot land while at sea

Landlubber
Someone who's not very skilled at sea

Me
Pirates say "me" instead of "my" or "I"

Methinks
I believe

Pillage
The act of looting or plundering

Plunder
Steal goods with force or pillage

Poop deck
Deck that's the farthest back and highest

Scurvy dog
Scoundrel

Scuttle
To sink a ship

Shiver me timbers!
An exclamation to express shock or surprise

Swashbuckling
Engaging in daring adventures with bravado

Ye
Pirates say "ye" instead of "you"

Yo ho ho!
Laughter

Treasure hunt

1.

Make a treasure chest by decorating a small cardboard box.
Put special messages or treats for your family inside.

2.

Draw a map of your house, your yard, or your neighborhood.
Hide the treasure chest and mark the location with an X on
the map you created.

3.

Ask your family to use the map to find the treasure!

Draw your
map here.

Trim out this page
and thank one of your
favorite teachers.

World
Teacher
Day

Dear .... ,

You're awesome

because:

....

....

....

I'll always remember
what
you said:

From you, I learned:

Thank you!

....

My Teacher and Me as Superheroes

Our superpowers are:

Our superhero names

If I were a teacher for a day, I would:

and

A new rule would be:

National Pumpkin Day

What does a pirate put
on a pumpkin?

A pumpkin patch!

Gourd or not a gourd?

Cantaloupe

☐ ☐
Yes No

Cucumber

☐ ☐
Yes No

Watermelon

☐ ☐
Yes No

Zucchini

☐ ☐
Yes No

Pumpkin

☐ ☐
Yes No

Crookneck squash

☐ ☐
Yes No

Tomato

☐ ☐
Yes No

Oh my gourd!
The world's biggest pumpkin weighed in at more than one ton.

Fruit or vegetable?
pumpkins are fruit!

Where are pumpkins grown?

They're grown on every continent except Antarctica. They've been in North America for 5,000 years. In the United States, Illinois produces the most pumpkins.

How did carving pumpkins for Halloween become a thing?

Irish immigrants brought the jack-o'-lantern tradition to America. Back in Ireland (starting hundreds of years ago), they carved potatoes or turnips. It's not easy to carve a turnip!

How many seeds are in a pumpkin?

Each pumpkin has about 500 seeds (give or take). They're full of fiber and protein. Try roasting them for a tasty, nutritious treat!

Sit a Spell

Set a timer for one minute.
See how many words you can come up with using the letters in the word

PUMPKIN

(grab a friend or two if you want to make it a competition).

One Great Pumpkin

Decorate it any way you like.

Sink or float?

Get different-sized pumpkins.
Fill a large container or bathtub with water.

The answer is on the back of the sticker page near the end of this book. (Don't peek. Try it first!)

1. **Hypothesize.**

Predict whether you think each pumpkin will sink or float in the water, and why.

2. **Experiment.**

Try it!

3. **Observe.**

What happened? Why?

World

Kindness

Day

Make a kindness box

1. Decorate a box.

2. Cut up some slips of paper.

3. Write an act of kindness— big or small—on each one.

4. Draw one slip from the box once a week (or more!) and keep kindness going.

Go on a hike, and pick up any trash you see.

Smile at everyone you see today.

Deliver a special drawing to a neighbor.

Write a thank-you note to your teacher.

Make treats and bring them to the local fire station.

Donate books to the library.

More ideas:

Breakfast table talk

How can you spread kindness today?

Who was kind to you yesterday?

How can you be a good friend today?

Take

a

Hike

Day

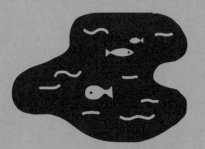

My Dream Hike

Draw it here.

Who I'd take with me

What's in my backpack

A snack I'd pack

Hike Hunt

Take note of what you find, or bring a camera to capture things as you go. Make copies for everyone, and see who finishes first!

Draw a bird you see.

Name it:

Collect 3 different types of leaves

(non-poisonous only, please).

☐

Find a unique rock.

☐

(Pocket it, unless it's not allowed.)

Spot what could very well be an animal's home.

☐

Spot a cool cloud.
Describe its shape:

Find a normal bug.
Give it an abnormal name:

Hello,
my name is

Spot something red:

Spot something pink:

Spot something yellow:

that starts with an "S."

Discover something

Find a flower.

What's something super-interesting you discovered?

Family goal

Come up with a goal to tackle as a family this month, or this year.
Give it a catchy name.

THE
HIKE
5
(take 5 family hikes)

THE
WHOA
2-0
(cover a total of 20 miles)

Plan how you'll celebrate together when you achieve your goal. Ice cream? Matching tees? Trip to Yellowstone?

Do you geocache?

Geocaching is a massive outdoor treasure hunt. There are millions of geocaches—containers holding small trinkets—hidden around the world at locations that have been posted online.

To add more adventure to your hike, try tracking down a geocache. When you find it, sign the log book, trade a trinket if you'd like, and then track its travels. (When we tried it, our tiny toy seal traveled from San Francisco to Denmark, Poland, Estonia, and Singapore!) Check out geocaching.com to get started.